ABOVE SEATTLE

by ROBERT CAMERON

A new collection of historical and original
aerial photographs of Seattle

with text by
EMMETT WATSON

CAMERON and COMPANY, San Francisco, California

TABLE OF CONTENTS

Putting together a book like Above Seattle can be enormously complex and requires the help of many friendly, even dedicated people. So, for their encouragement and expertise, I thank the following:

Hatsuro Aizawa, Fred Brack, Robert Burger, Rick Caldwell, Anthony Cameron, Madelaine Cassidy, Jim DiLeonardo, Chuck & Pam Easter, Robert Ekstrand, Richard Engeman, John Goy, Linda Henry, Tina Hodge, Tom Lubbesmeyer, Alicemarie Mutrux, Patricia O'Grady, Paul Skinner, Bill Thaxton, Linda Sullivan Tung and Jerome Vloeberghs.

Special thanks should go to Otto Lang whose knowledge, and consultation were invaluable.
Thanks too to Dean and Jim Leong for the same.

In the air and on the ground we were greatly assisted by: the various Air Controllers; the Seattle Fire Department and last and most important the expert piloting by Randy O'Neill and Ted Potter, masters of their craft.

For assistance in researching the historical aerial photography, acknowledgement is made to:

Seattle Museum of History and Industry for pages 8, 10, 24, 32, 36, 44, 46, 70, 86, 94, 114, 139
Boeing Historical Archives for page 96
University of Washington Libraries, Special Collections for pages 6, 22, 156
Seattle Times News and Everett Herald for pages 150, 152, 154

National Aeronautics and Space Administration for pages 5, 73, 144

CAMERON and COMPANY

543 Howard Street   San Francisco, California 94105 USA   415/777-5582

Library of Congress Catalog Number: 94-094006
Above Seattle ISBN 0-918684-41-2
© 1994 by Robert W. Cameron and Company, Inc. All rights reserved.

First Printing, 1994

Book design by
JANE OLAUG KRISTIANSEN

Color processing by The New Lab, San Francisco and Ivey Seright, Seattle
Cameras by Pentax
Color Separations and Printing in Hong Kong

Viewed from the air, Seattle has an hour-glass figure, pinched at its downtown waist by two large bodies of water, Elliott Bay and Lake Washington. This shape calls to mind that of Lillian Russell, the buxom actress who dazzled the world from 1881 to 1908. The era is important. While Lillian consorted with Diamond Jim Brady on New York's turn-of-the-century fast track, Seattle was a distant, little-known seaport, a brawling, tough crossroads frontier town, whose chief claim to fame was being "the jumping off point" for the 1898 Yukon gold rush.

Indeed, it was the expertise of Alaska miners that made Seattle into a city. Too many hills? We'll sluice them down, by god. Starting early in the century and continuing into the 1930s — using high-powered hoses and techniques developed in Alaska gold mining — city fathers performed 62 "regrades" to level Seattle's hilly terrain. Millions of cubic yards were washed into Elliott Bay to create a deep-water harbor and fill in tidelands. Dozens of in-city sawmills raised a cacophony as islands rose, rivers split, canals and harbors formed. Much of what you see in Bob Cameron's remarkable aerial views of Seattle is man-made. A great industrial area, even the famous Kingdome itself, rests on ground reclaimed from the sea. In this book, too, is a view of Harbor Island, within a stone's throw of the city's skyscrapers. Harbor Island, the locus of Seattle's immense trade with Pacific Rim countries, was created out of silt from nearby hills; a river, the Duwamish, was divided to provide deep-water shipping five miles inland. We've got world-class mud, and we know that to do with it.

And water everywhere! From the sky, from the rivers, from Puget Sound and the lakes, water means islands, inlets, harbors, breakwaters, marinas, great freighters, tugboats, ferries and perhaps more privately owned pleasure boats than any other American city.

There are no fewer than 112 bridges inside Seattle's city limits, including three that float on concrete pontoons across Lake Washington. Of the 91 square miles of land within the city, 80 percent are surrounded by water. Puget Sound, an inland salt-water body, stretches from Olympia and Tacoma north to the Strait of Juan de Fuca, a lighthouse flicker away from Canada. When Seattle's Chittenden Locks were completed in 1914, thus equalizing the 33-foot difference in height between Puget Sound and Lake Union and 20-mile long Lake Washington, the builders and power brokers were ecstatic. "We will make Lake Washington an industrial giant, the Pittsburgh of the West," they boasted.

"Like hell you will," the people said.

They said it by buying up would-be lakefront industrial sites for homesites. Some wealthy, some not, Seattleites settled along the city's shorelines — 193 miles of waterfront, including 100 miles of fresh-water mooring space. Could a city like this ever have an identity crisis?

The short answer: yes. As the half-century mark passed, the joke was, "When the end of the world comes, Seattle will have one more year." This was meant to underscore the city's backwardness, its damp distance from the mainline of America's fads, fashion and energy.

Seattle chafed at its anonymity. It was America's best-kept urban secret, isolated by geography and insulated by a mind-set of chauvinism. Everything east of the mighty Cascade range and Mt. Rainier was "them," and some people liked it that way.

Then, on a bright, clear August day in 1955, a moment of change occurred. Some 200,000 people witnessed it, but few probably understood that they saw. This throng had gathered ashore and on pleasure boats to watch the annual hydroplane races on Lake Washington — yet another of Seattle's festive water celebrations. Somewhere out over the Puget Sound a totally new airplane was being wrung out by Tex Johnston, the famed test-pilot of every American jet produced since World War II and himself a willing captive of Seattle. Now he was pushing the limits of a new jet designated as the Dash-80, a product of Boeing, which had begun in "a little red barn" on Lake Union during World War I. Up there at 12,000 feet, Tex Johnston and his crew could see all the glory of the Pacific Northwest, the glory you will see in this book. The vista: Two great mountain ranges, the ocean, the shoreline, the lakes, the rivers, the harbors, the boats, the skyline of Seattle. It was a panorama to half-blind the most casual of visitors.

As planned, Tex brought the Dash-80 down low over Lake Washington. Spectators craned their necks for a first glimpse of Boeing's heralded new airplane. Silence fell on the huge crowd, which included, by special invitation, the chiefs of all the world's major airlines. And then, in a dramatic departure from the script written by Boeing's brass, Tex slow-rolled the giant jet only 200 feet above the water, as if it were nothing more than a little military aircraft. While blood drained from his bosses' cheeks ashore, Tex returned and repeated the swashbuckling gesture, delivering emphatic notice that the jet-age had arrived.

Progeny of the prototype Dash-80 became known as Boeing 707s — America's first passenger jets. More than a thousand of them were produced in Boeing's Puget Sound factories, and millions of middle-income people flew for the first time on "that plane from Seattle." Johnston would later drawl, "We have shrunk the world by a factor of two." And, incidentally, carried Seattle's name around the globe.

Still, it wasn't enough. The city's identity crisis persisted. Seattle drifted along at the edge of America's consciousness. Underneath the placid surface, however, a mysterious alchemy was taking place, an explosive combination of local big thinkers and bright, restless newcomers attracted by the area's natural beauty. All this energy seemed to come together in the 1980s, when Seattle burst onto the world scene...as, well, a better place to be, a place of limitless commercial, intellectual, recreational and artistic possibilities — as well as a great place to raise a family. And a place where the imperative of the '90s, ethnic and racial accommodation, is bringing new vitality to a city where once a stodgy, lily-white power structure held absolute sway.

Much of Seattle's newly-discovered greatness was home-grown. A young bond lawyer, Jim Ellis, rallied the citizens to save Lake Washington from pollution. He exhorted his region to provide money for more parks and greenery; out of this effort came the Kingdome and major league sports. Ellis and his supporters also brought forth a convention center and a downtown park — both built over a soulless freeway. A local architectual firm, Jones and Jones, designed a revolutionary type of zoo, now imitated all over the world.

Nordstrom, founded by a Northwest family, became a national force in fashion retailing. Eddie Bauer, once a little downtown sporting goods store, set national standards for recreational outdoor clothing. Jim Whittaker, a home-grown mountaineer and the first American to ascend Mt. Everest, helped establish a co-op called REI, now a famous outdoors outfitter. Two native computer whizzes, Bill Gates and Paul Allen, barely out of Lakeside High School, founded Microsoft, which exploded into the world's largest software company. Local theater groups nurtured plays that went east to become Broadway hits. Movie companies became common sights on city streets. Grunge Rock (forgive us) burst out of Seattle's little clubs and swept across the country.

And, without even trying, Seattle became, of all things, the coffee capital of America. Three young advertising people, with nothing more in mind than to create a better brew, founded a tiny coffee shop in the Pike Place Market called Starbucks. Now Starbucks shops are hop-scotching across the nation, along with several other Seattle specialty coffee roasters. Visitors are bewildered by the city's ubiquitous espresso stands; we have more espresso carts than cash machines, and some people wonder if Seattle's new prominence is nothing more than an outsized caffeine jag.

In short, Seattle has become a kind of "happening" — in food, in lifestyle, in the arts, in high tech, in ideas. For whatever reason, the magic glass slipper fits. In the national consciousness, Seattle is the belle of America's urban ball. Midnight seems far away.

— *E.W.*

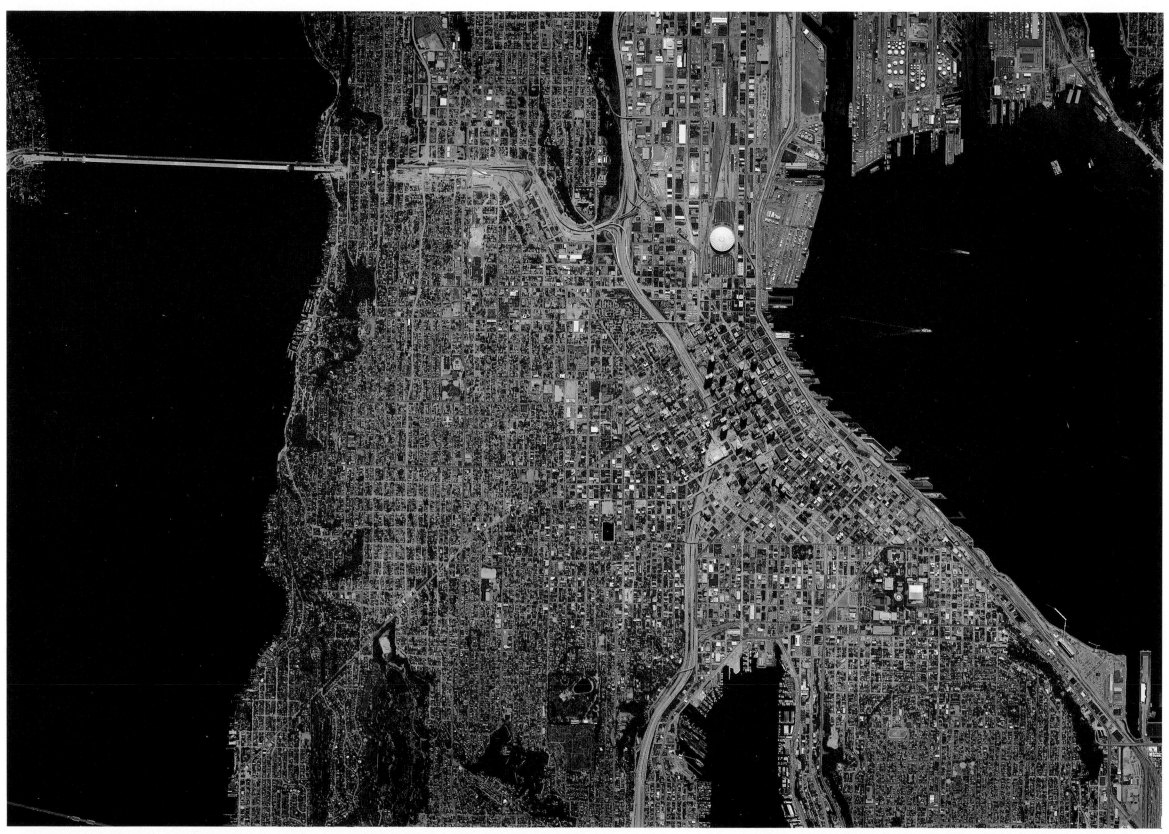

(Opposite) There she is, in all her glitzy glory, the once ugly, rain-soaked fishing and lumbering town, now voted by many national magazines as "America's most liveable city." The piers to the left of the jumbo ferry were once an honest, hard-working waterfront. Today they're a row of restaurants, bauble shops, T-shirt emporiums and tourist-catching souvenir places. The old working waterfront is now far south, along Harbor Island. On the right is the white peaked tower of the L.C. Smith Building, erected in 1914 as "the tallest building west of Chicago." The elegant old Smith Tower is dwarfed, but still proud, next to the black 76-story Columbia Center building, more than twice as tall as Seattle's signature Space Needle. Natives are sometimes wary of the great, intimidating skyscrapers that make up Seattle's skyline. But there it is, modernity run amok, the image somehow softened by Lake Washington and the Cascade Mountain range in the backgi that "lies well in the arms of the land."

This NASA photo from space presents a dramatic view of how Seattle is pinched at the waist by water. Elliott Bay is on the right, Lake Washington on the left (note the floating bridge). Also shown is Lake Union (at bottom), which nestles close to downtown. This perspective is a dramatic demonstration of the water-oriented city Seattle is. The red-tinted sections are really the city's abundant greenery, no small reason Seattle calls itself the Emerald City.

THIS BIRDS EYE VIEW OF SEATTLE HAS BEEN PREPARED ESPECIALLY BY

LLEWELLYN, DODGE & CO.

LLEWELLYN-DODGE BUILDING SEATTLE, WASH.

MINING & REAL ESTATE BROKERS
AND AUCTIONEERS.

We take this opportunity of thanking the enterprising gentlemen who have contributed to the success of this Birds Eye View of Seattle

Respectfully

Llewellyn Dodge & Co

Llewellyn Dodge Building

INCORPORATED. AUTHORIZED CAPITAL, $250,000. PAID UP CAPITAL, $100,000.

DOES A GENERAL BANKING BUSINESS. COLLECTIONS A SPECIALTY.

THE BANK OF COMMERCE.

SEATTLE, 1889.

Copyrighted by Llewellyn, Dodge & Co. Seattle, 1889.

Lith. by Schmidt L. & I. Co. S. Y.

Pub. by The Elliott Pub. Co., 120 Sutter St. S.F.

Seattle's massive skyline, with Lake Washington in the background, then the Cascade mountain range shrouded in clouds some 60 miles away, is the city's statement of its greatness. The ancient image of the waterfront shows the city as it once was. From the dark line to the waterfront is the area destroyed by fire in 1889. The water and tidelands to the right are now completely filled and form the city's industrial area. Built upon this fill are much of Pioneer Square and Seattle's indoor stadium, the Kingdome.

6

The 42-story SMITH TOWER, built in 1914, was once America's tallest building west of Chicago. Though dwarfed today by modern skyscrapers, the pointed tower, visible on the right edge of downtown, maintains its regal dignity. In the earlier 1933 photograph, the Smith Tower rises unrivaled. The water in the background is Lake Washington.

Somewhere on an Alaska beach is the battered, abused remnant of the KALAKALA, the tear-shaped oddity shown here in 1935 along Seattle's waterfront. The Kalakala was designed by one of America's avant garde industrial designers, Norman Bel Geddes. It was the brain-child of Capt. Alex Peabody, head of the Black Ball Line, a private ferry company later bought by the State of Washington, which runs the Puget Sound ferry system. In her time and in her day, the Kalakala ("Flying Cloud") was world renowned. She was as much a Seattle symbol as the Space Needle is today.

The Kalakala was built over the burned-out hull of the crack San Francisco Bay ferry Peralta, launched in 1927. Capt. Peabody bought the hulk, had it towed to Seattle, and commissioned Bel Geddes, famed for his stage sets, to design something that would take Seattle into "the streamlined age." The Kalakala cruised at 15 knots and vibrated like a foot massager.

The contemporary view of Seattle's waterfront shows two modern ferries at the city's ferry terminal.

That thing you are looking at is called a hyperbolic paraboloid concrete dome, and now don't you feel better for knowing that? THE KINGDOME, its official name (after King County), was conceived in controversy, perhaps a dozen lawsuits, and suggested alternatives that bordered on lunacy. One magnificent proposal was to build Seattle's covered stadium so it would float on Elliott Bay. Nobody thought to worry about seasick sports fans.

The Kingdome has hosted major league baseball and NFL football, paper airplane contests, car-wrecking extravaganzas and one record-breaking attendance (see Guinness Book of World Records) of 103,152 for a two-day Christmas party put on by the Boeing Co. Seattleites call it "the orange juice squeezer." The Rev. Billy Graham brought major league religion in 1976; the Reverend still holds the single-event Kingdome attendance record of 74,000 souls, saved and unsaved.

SEATTLE CENTER. Here you see the site of the World's Fair in 1962. In the center is the Coliseum, home to trade shows, circuses and Seattle's NBA SuperSonics; nearby is a carnival-like Fun Forest. In the upper far right are spindly legs that go up to become the Space Needle. A bit further to the right are the spirals of the Pacific Science Center, designed by Minouro Yamasaki. Off to the left of the Coliseum is the greenish yellow Bagley Wright Theatre and beyond that the white-roofed brick Opera House; next to that, High School Memorial Stadium. Between the stadium and the Coliseum is the great Center fountain. The Coliseum holds one major distinction: it is the only such place in the world where an NBA basketball had to be postponed because of rain. The roof leaked.

SORRENTO HOTEL. This Italian Rennaissance hotel, desiged by Harlan Thomas, first dean at the University of Washington's architecture school, has been a Seattle landmark for 84 years. Its opening in 1909 coincided with the Alaska-Yukon Exposition. Thomas also designed the Corner Public Market Building in the city's famed Pike Place Market. The seven-story Sorrento was given a $4.5 million facelift in 1981. Each room is designed differently, and the Sorrento now ranks among the best of Seattle's small luxury hotels.

Since 1924, when it opened, THE OLYMPIC HOTEL has been Seattle's grand dame of social gatherings, and boosters claimed it as "bigger and more important than the Klondike Gold Rush." The Olympic was originally built on public subscription — a fund-raiser involving 3,000 rain-soaked patriots who raised the $5.5 million needed. Over the years, the Olympic has hosted six presidents, some kings and emperors and a few leftover dukes and duchesses. Where the Olympic sits today was once the University of Washington — indeed, the university still owns the property under the hotel.

In 1980, the Olympic, by then on the National Register of Historic Places, was given major surgery, both cosmetic and physical, by the Four Seasons of Toronto and Urban Investment of Chicago. The Olympic featured small rooms, some 756 of them, known as "Willy Loman rooms." The investors reduced the number of rooms to 451 and called it the Four Seasons Olympic. The operation took some $60 million and nearly two years to complete. It is once again Seattle's most elegant hotel.

(Opposite) Mark Tobey, the late great artist, called the PIKE PLACE MARKET "the soul of Seattle." The city saved its soul in 1971 when citizens rose up in righteous balloting, voting to save the ratty, run-down public market from developers. The Market, spread along Seattle's downtown, attracts millions of visitors, native and tourist, each year. It is a Rabelasian strip of vegetable stands, fish markets, shops and restaurants, each approved by a Market Historical Commission. The soul of Seattle is now regarded by its citizens as hallowed ground.

From a height of 800 feet, Cameron's camera does an eyes-down view of Seattle's signature SPACE NEEDLE, which soars 607.88 feet into the sky. The Space Needle, built to withstand 150-mile-per-hour winds, has 24 lightning rods, a revolving restaurant, and is embedded in 3,700 tons of concrete. The Monorail, America's first such passenger-carrying, single-track device, carries 400,000 people annually to and from downtown and Seattle Center.

(Opposite) As few others ever have, Bob Cameron's laser-like artistry captures this dramatic view of Seattle's visual signature, the towering, triple-legged SPACE NEEDLE, a legacy of the city's World's Fair of 1962. In the foreground is the Science Center, a place of constant, public-welcomed exhibits of modern science. Lake Union is in the background and beyond that the University of Washington.

THE UNIVERSITY CLUB at the corner of Boren and Madison is probably Seattle's most exclusive club. But don't take that too seriously. Its membership is not allowed to exceed 250 (no women allowed) and its red-roofed three-story wood building is nothing to make an architect faint with joy. This all-male bastion of businessmen is discouraged from discussing business within its undistinguished walls. Men, well-heeled or -connected, just enjoy each other. As one woman journalist wrote, "The University Club has neither fine athletic facilities nor elegant decor ... it is simply a place where a select group of men meet to enjoy each other's company, away from people of differing race, religion, sex or social class. As it is, the organization's selectivity and secrecy give it a certain glamour."

Edward E. Carlson, once manager of the RAINIER CLUB, later head of United Airlines, described the Tudor-style "clubhouse" as "a luncheon club for the Establishment, the place where the deals were made." The Rainier Club, a bastion of Seattle's business class, is a dark brick edifice pictured here among the glass, steel and aluminum towers that surround it on 4th and Marion. It has a look of inviting warmth, but only a few are invited to partake of its good food and clubby exclusiveness. It was ever so. In its early days it banned women from its premises, and a 1962 survey revealed that almost half of the 260 members were aged 60 or more. Unless it loosened its membership requirements, the club was in danger of dying itself out of existence. Requirements were then relaxed. Right behind the Rainier Club is the red-roofed United Methodist Church. This sanctuary was built in 1909. The United Methodists are the oldest Christian Community in Seattle, started on Dec. 4, 1853.

(Opposite) Using a "fisheye" lens, Cameron took this whimsical view of Seattle's severely vertical skyline. Enjoy, but don't take it seriously.

Seattle's newest boat haven in ELLIOTT BAY MARINA. Close to the city's downtown, it accommodates 1,200 pleasure boats. The white building in the background is a grain terminal, whose view-blocking size causes seizures of outrage among Queen Anne Hill householders.

(Opposite) Not so imposing from the outside, Seattle's AQUARIUM (Pier 59) is the tourist-conscious central waterfront's big draw. Inside is a maze of illuminated displays. Fish of all kinds – sharks, snapper, octopi and salmon coming home to spawn. Tiny salmon, released from the aquarium, return in 3-4 years, as if by radar. These tired, sometimes battered, natives can be seen through glass-enclosed fish ladders. There are convincing re-creations of intertidal and coastal ecosystems. Also inside is the Omnidome Theatre with depictions of nature's underwater spectacles. You can spend an entire day in this place and only your feet will get tired.

This 1910 "moonscape" photo (above) shows DENNY HILL being sluiced down into Elliott Bay when Seattle was a raw and very muddy place. In the far distance can be seen the twin towers of St. James Cathedral. The moonscape has now been replaced by the Space Needle, Seattle Center, office buildings and rows of high-rise downtown apartments and condominiums. The St. James towers are now lost behind the city's skyscrapers.

As pictured over a span of 70 years, Seattle's DOWN-TOWN has changed primarily in terms of verticality.

After what seemed like years of caterwauling over location, size, cost and whether we needed it at all, the WASHINGTON STATE CONVENTION AND TRADE CENTER was finished in 1988. Aesthetically, it's a beauty, because it covers a portion of the ugly I-5 freeway corridor through the city's heart. Next to it is seven-acre Freeway Park, with plazas, fountains and pools — also over the freeway. It is now one of Seattle's busiest places.

Lake all other large cities, Seattle is blessed (or cursed) with cloverleaf freeway exchanges which become exasperating gridlocks. Fortunately for these car-borne prisoners, mobile phones are catching on.

(Opposite) In a region blessed by much water and dozens of islands, you would not think Seattle would need to build its own island. But Seattle may be the hydrology capital of the world; it has sluiced down hills, covered tide flats, dug canals and – to be sure – built islands. Here is HARBOR ISLAND, part of the city's great port, where most of the shipping occurs. Harbor Island, 420 square acres of it, was made from the inoffensive and otherwise peaceful Duwamish River, flowing into Elliott Bay. It is built entirely of dredged silt. The great dredging process split the river in two – down one side flows the "east waterway," down the other, "west waterway." This silt-dredging deepened and expanded the big freighter ship capacity of Seattle's waterfront. Deep draft ships can now go 5.3 miles up the river, adding yet more acres to the Port of Seattle's capacity to handle cargo. The huge orange "praying mantises" are part of the Port's squadron of 23 such giant cranes. The Port of Seattle is the nation's fourth largest container port. It tops any other U.S. port in container tonnage exports to Asia.

It cannot be said too often, although many Seattleites have tried, that Harbor Island and other Seattle berthing points are 260 nautical miles closer to Japan than Bay Area ports. The port is 563 miles closer than Long Beach or Los Angeles. Assuming an average speed of 20 knots, Seattle has a 15-hour sailing advantage over Oakland-San Francisco and a 30-hour advantage over Southern California ports. Seattle is also, the boosters like to point out, the "short cut" to ports in Alaska.

Should you feel poorly, Seattle is the place to be. It has a plethora of hospitals, clinics, laboratories and research centers, many of them located on FIRST HILL, known to Seattleites as "Pill Hill." Here are two views of Pill Hill. In the foreground opposite is Harborview Hospital, well named for its sweeping view of Puget Sound to the left, or west. In the background is the cluster of light-colored buildings that comprise Swedish Medical Center. Among other medical facilities in this area is the famous Fred Hutchinson Cancer Research Center, which honors a native-son baseball player who died of the disease. (The Center has a new, giant addition on Lake Union.) (Above) Looking west, is a closer view of the Swedish complex. Elsewhere in Seattle is the massive University of Washington Medical Center and the Children's Hospital and Medical Center, one of the world's great child-treatment centers, largely promoted and financed by women activists. In few cities anywhere do commuting doctors cause such traffic jams.

Located close to Seattle's downtown and adjacent to the Swedish Medical Center is SEATTLE UNIVERSITY. Its urban campus has grown to 52 acres. SU is one of 28 Jesuit colleges in the United States, and as Seattle College it became (in 1933) the first Jesuit college to enroll women. Student demographics reveal that women students outnumber men – 2,563 to 2,267. Before it deemphasized basketball some 20 years ago, Seattle University was a national power.

This imposing brick building and tower dominate the PROVIDENCE MEDICAL CENTER a few blocks east of Seattle's famed "Pill Hill." It is the oldest hospital in Seattle. Providence was in several locations before its large new building was completed in 1910. Founded by the Sisters of Providence, the hospital grew from a time when Seattle had a population of 3,533 people, including five blacksmiths, 24 lawyers, six barbers, 30 saloons, three dealers in hides and furs, nine hotels and three theatres. Today's magnificent facility has a personnel complement of more than 3,000 and a bed capacity of 565.

(Opposite) A tidy little nine-hole golf course once occupied part of the impressive UNIVERSITY OF WASHINGTON MEDICAL CENTER, fronting on Portage Bay. Opened in 1959 with 60 beds, the then UW Hospital was elevated in rank to the University of Washington Medical Center in 1989. On the cutting edge of research, the medical center now has 450 patient beds, some 400 faculty doctors and more than 1,200 employees. Connoisseurs of symbolism should read no exotic meaning into the perfect concrete-and-grass circle in the foreground. It is the entrance to a large underground parking garage.

31

This is a view, looking east, of Seattle's University District. The UNIVERSITY OF WASHINGTON is at the top, Husky Stadium's "wings" soar on the shore of Lake Washington and the University Medical Center complex can be seen in the upper right. Above is a view of the University in 1932. Note not only the growth of the University and the football stadium but the dramatic growth of the commercial district around the University.

(Opposite) Slightly to the left and down toward Portage Bay is UNIVERSITY AVENUE, simply called "The Ave" by students and public alike. Seattle's skyline is in the distance. The greenery to the left is the beginning of the University of Washington campus. Tucked in front of the dominating Safeco Insurance Building is the former Edmund Meany Hotel, named after a distinguished UW professor. It is now called Meany Tower Hotel. At the left-center of the picture on The Ave is a brown apartment building – the Wilsonian – distinguished in Seattle history because Bertha K. Landes, the first woman mayor of any large American city, once lived there. Mrs. Landes, who served one two-year term, became a national celebrity because she shut down the wild waterfront town and went on to become the best mayor Seattle ever had. They admiringly called her "Big Bertha."

Gone, long gone, will be the cramped, sterile – and cruel – cages with cement floors. WOODLAND PARK ZOO (the left side of the green area) is already considered the nation's model for creative, natural animal habitat. When completed in 1997, the zoo will have no fewer than eight "bioclimatic zones" that replicate, as far as possible, divisions of the world created by natural climate and vegetation. Woodland Park Zoo is revolutionary, hailed by international experts (including the late Diane Fossey) as an example of how zoos should be developed. Bond issue money and private donations have raised, and intend to raise, more than $51 million to complete its natural setting. As small concrete enclosures give way to spacious, open exhibits, visitors feel part of the animal world around them. The body of water is Green Lake.

VOLUNTEER PARK. The name of this elegant view park means just that — it was named after volunteers of the Spanish-American War. You can find almost anything here — statues, the Seattle Asian Art Museum, a conservatory, and a water tower you can climb until breathless. Flowers, picnics, kite-flying tournaments, rock concerts, bike races and sometimes open-air sex are part of Volunteer Park amusements. Monuments, statues and sculptures commemorate almost everything — from the stately William Seward, the Eager Beaver Gardeners and the sinking of the Maine. Once known as City Park, the splendid grounds became Volunteer Park in 1901 at the suggestion of one J. Willis Sayre, himself a Spanish-American War veteran. He suggested the park name be changed to honor all veterans who volunteered for service against Spain. Mr. Sayre, a longtime Seattle editor, reporter and film reviewer, set a speed record in 1903 by circling the globe by various conveyances in 54 days, nine hours and 42 minutes. He paid his way with $800 in $20 gold pieces. Nobody thought to honor him with a statue. As can be seen from the 1934 photo (above), Volunteer Park has avoided change.

Nestled in alongside a luxury apartment and two white NOAA research ships is another Seattle signature – HOUSEBOATS. Houseboats are uniquely Seattle and they are old as the city itself. The first houseboats were built by workers in logging camps, curious, one-story, jerry-built lodgings, built on rafts to follow logs down the river. Later they were used by families as permanent homes on Lake Union (this view) and the south shore of Portage Bay (opposite view), then for the bohemian crowd and university students. Bootleggers of Prohibition used them freely and so did commercial fishermen. By the late 1930s there were 2,000 of them. Later houseboat dwellers fought against city bureaucrats determined to "clean up the lake." In recent years, however, the houseboats have won their right to survival. Many are of vintage "sprung roof" design, but a few are architecural masterpieces, valued at more than $500,000. Lately, many houseboats have become "condo-ized," buying their own waterfront moorage spaces. Today there are only about 485 houseboats left in Seattle.

This sidehill acreage is DANNY WOO GARDEN (named after a local businessman), a prized posession of Seattle's sizeable Asian community. It is a one-acre terraced garden with approximately 80 garden plots for elderly citizens in the International District. This "P-Patch" public garden is one of 30 in Seattle. P-Patch gardeners annually donate some eight tons of fresh vegetables to local food banks.

FREEWAY PARK has been called "the ultimate oxymoron" – a park built smack on top of the downtown freeway. How can you make a freeway and a park live together? But it works. This jungle-like downtown park was built in conjunction with the big downtown Washington State Convention Center, much of it also built over the freeway. The little park is carefully watered, barbered and tended, so this urban retreat, with its winding paths and greenery, is a delightful oasis among skyscrapers, where hundreds go to eat their lunches and bask in the sun.

HAMMERING MAN. When the Seattle Art Museum moved its principal collections downtown from an undersized building in Volunteer Park, Robert Venturi was architect of the new building. Sculptor Jonathan Borofsky was chosen to produce the centerpiece. Venturi's design, after much squabbling with the construction firm, was generally applauded. Borofsky gave the city a huge, black 48-foot tribute to working people called "Hammering Man." But the project wouldn't have a Seattle flavor unless something bad happened — like sunken bridges, a collapsed UW Stadium, and all such as that. "Man" crashed when a sling broke as the 13-ton piece was being hoisted into place. Damage was considerable, although not as much as some members of Seattle's arts community would have hoped for. A year later the Big Guy (he cost $450,000) was installed and, since 1992, his hammering arm has moved up and down four times a minute ever since. Critics of "Man" eagerly await a good windstorm.

GREEN LAKE is an in-city amenity, a 342-acre playground for low-key boating, windsurfing and shell races. It is 2.8 miles around, and if you don't like crowds, stay away from Green Lake. Some 10,000 people visit Green Lake on a sunny weekend day. It is so popular that walkers, joggers, skateboarders and bicyclists have been injured on its 12-foot-wide path. Some 1.5 million people visit Green Lake each year. It is Seattle's most popular on-the-cheap recreational area.

(Opposite) Seattle is a moveable feast of views, none more enticing than this one, looking north across LAKE UNION.

THE SEATTLE TENNIS CLUB is now 104 years old, having been founded in 1890 as the Olympic Tennis Club. It moved from a high hill, at Boren and Madison, where the ultra exclusive University Club now stands. On March 24, 1896, the members changed the club's name to Seattle Tennis Club. It can rightfully boast of being Seattle's "oldest family club." By 1910, the population of Seattle burgeoned to a border-busting 237,194 and by 1920, pinched for space, the Seattle Tennis Club moved to the shores of Lake Washington — on property that was breathtakingly beautiful and would become equally expensive. The photograph above was taken in 1936.

THE SEATTLE YACHT CLUB'S clubhouse, complete with lighthouse on top, was built in 1920. Today it symbolizes what The Saturday Evening Post in 1953 called "the boating capital of the world." Seattle is a city so enthralled with the briney life that its Yellow Pages contain about two dozen pages under "boat." The roots of this mania go deep; the Yacht Club traces its beginnings to 1875, about a generation after the city was founded. Any aspiring new member absolutely must own a boat in order to join. Any invited guest can, however, snitch a book of matches bearing the legend, "BGDYCITWWW." Members are proud to translate: "Best goddam yacht club in the whole wide world." Above is a view of the club in 1938.

The north section of Seattle, located on Capitol Hill, is a series of old neighborhoods, practically drowned in greenery. In the foreground is ST. JOSEPH'S CHURCH, established in 1907. In the lower right is St. Joseph's School. The dome in the background is Holy Names Academy, an all-girls school, ninth to 12th grade.

(Below) This is ST. DEMETRIOS, a beautiful Orthodox Greek Church, near the Montlake District and the University of Washington, which opened on March 31, 1963. The architect was Paul Thiry, the principal architect for the Seattle World's Fair of 1962, who executed the Byzantine-style design, so much a part of ancient Greek tradition.

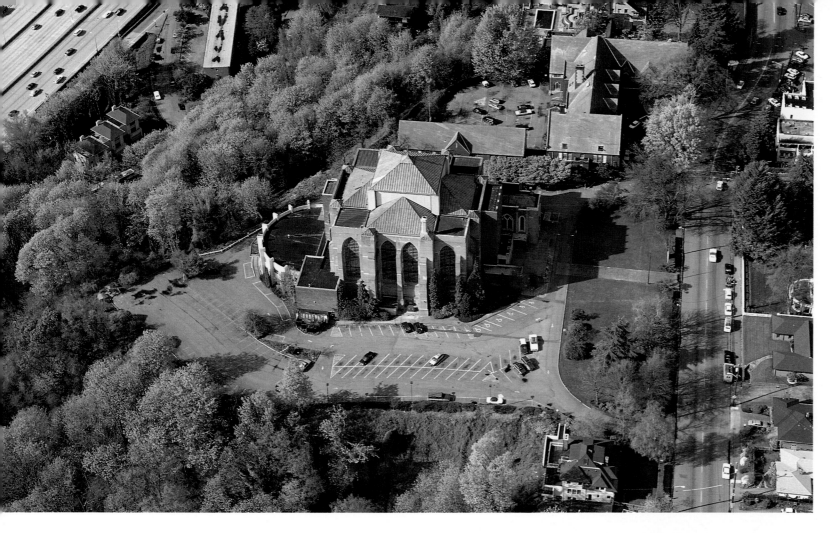

Conceived in boom years of the 1920s, ST. MARK'S CATHEDRAL went broke and closed its doors about 10 years after its first worship on April 25, 1931. Red-faced Seattle Episcopalians had a bankrupt building on their hands. At one time it was grandly said that St. Mark's was the largest pour of concrete in Washington State – second only to Grand Coulee Dam. But for a long time after the cathedral closed in 1941, there was a sign on its weedy grounds: "This Church For Sale." It was the powerful and feared Teamster Union leader, Dave Beck, who saved the church. At a civic luncheon, Beck, along with brewer Emil Sick, did not ask for money. He demanded it. Merchants, bankers, tavern keepers, race-track operators, assorted Protestant, Catholics, Jews and agnostics were hit for $85,000 in a civic drama that saved the church.

The cruciform-shaped ST. JAMES CATHEDRAL, with its twin towers and vaulting dome, was once one of the largest buildings in Seattle. It opened its doors on Dec. 15, 1907. Today it looks small facing Seattle's great skyscrapers and "Pill Hill," or First Hill, behind it. Less than nine years after it opened, Seattle was hit by the 1916 snowstorm; 15 tons of snow collapsed the central portion of the roof. Rebuilt at great cost, the Cathedral later made radio history by being the first church in the West to broadcast a service.

(Opposite) MORMON TEMPLE. There are now Mormon temples serving 23 countries worldwide; 22 of the temples are in the United States, including this one, located near the I-90 freeway and slightly east of Bellevue. This strikingly beautiful temple was designed by architect Emil Fetzer. It is said that Fetzer was so taken by the buttresses of the Cathedral of Notre Dame in Paris that he wanted to use them here. When the Temple opened in 1980 a month-long open house drew 259,282 visitors. The Seattle Temple of Church of Jesus Christ of Latter Day Saints is used by an estimated 250,000 Mormons in Washington, Oregon, Western Idaho, Western Canada and Alaska.

49

LESCHI PARK district, along Lake Washington, was named after Chief Leschi who allegedly led Nisqually tribal attacks against Seattle's white pioneers. Leschi, the focus of white hatred, was shamefully hanged, despite evidence of his innocence. In the distance is the Smith Tower and Yesler Way, where once cable cars ran from downtown and connected with cross-lake ferries.

(Opposite) MADISON PARK. This upscale neighborhood, close to posh, was once Seattle's favorite lakeside vacation grounds. Many of the homes are redone cottages. A racetrack once flourished here. Today's population is a mix of young professionals and retired people. East Madison, a long, hilly street stretching to the heart of downtown, was once serviced by a cable car and a ferry that took people east of Lake Washington.

Established in 1926, the SAND POINT COUNTRY CLUB overlooks the north part of Lake Washington, yet it's definitely an in-city private golf club. The challenging 6,000-yard layout has 400 golfing and 325 social members.

BROADMOOR GOLF CLUB, certainly among the first to be lined by prestigious homes, is only a few minutes east of downtown Seattle. When it opened in 1927, the cost to join was $110. Today new members must buy a single share of stock from another member for roughly $60,000 to $70,000. Memberships are held to 400. A short but demanding course, Broadmoor has hosted dozens of top tournaments, both men's and women's. In the Seattle Open of 1945, Byron Nelson shot a 259, 21 under Broadmoor's par. He won $2,500 in war bonds. Nestled next to Seattle's nature-rich Arboretum, Broadmoor also played host to a coyote in 1982. Members were warned not to pet him.

(Opposite) GAS WORKS PARK. Cities can be lucky. This small park, at the north end of Lake Union, was once an ugly old gas works, with no money to tear it down. Instead, somebody came up with the bright idea of stripping it down as much as possible, trucking in soil, then leaving a sort of metallugical sculpture from the old heap. Grass was planted, paths put in; now people can stand atop the 60-foot-high mound and admire the city skyline across Lake Union to the south. It may be one of Seattle's most breathtaking vistas. Gas Works park has become a playbarn for kids, a site for kiting and picnics; it attracts all ages, the picnic-prone, rock bands. Nowhere else in Seattle is the natural "action" of the city more visibly apparent — boats, airplanes, houseboats, sailing races; easy access, great kite flying and swimming.

LAKE VIEW, atop yet another of Seattle's hills with an incredible view of Puget Sound, lakes, forests and two mountain ranges, is a place where nobody can get out or nobody can get in. Under its gravestones are most of Seattle's pioneers. They include names like Boren, Yesler, Kinnear, Meydenbauer, Phinney, McGilvra, Denny — the kind who get streets named after them. And, of course, Dr. David Swinton Maynard, who may have been one of the town's first drunks, certainly its first doctor and perhaps its greatest benefactor. Lake View is an equal opportunity cemetery. Buried among whites are hundreds of blacks, Chinese and Japanese. Jew, Catholic and Protestant lie side by side. Princess Angeline, the daughter of Chief Seattle, is buried here. "The Sleeping Dragon" came to rest in Lake View — Lee Jung Fan, known as Bruce Lee, the legendary martial arts master, is buried here. Beside him is his son, Brandon Lee, recently killed on a movie-set shooting accident.

THE WASHINGTON PARK ARBORETUM is an incredible 172.5-acre park in the heart of Seattle. It accomodates bikers, nature lovers, swimmers, canoeists and far too many cars. For starters, visitors can ogle, touch and feel great Douglas Fir, Western hemlock and Western red cedar – and go on from there to more than 4,000 different species of trees, flowers, shrubs, herbs and vines. The Arboretum is a melange of pathways, swamplands, lily pads and pathways, corrupted by a few freeway pillars that approach the Evergreen Point Floating Bridge. It nestles next to the exclusive Broadmoor Golf Club and one nature-lover calls it "the shape of a giant squid, with boulevards and pathways along the contours of its body." The Arboretum is owned by the city of Seattle but no lumbering civic bureaucracy could do it justice. This marvelous urban park is managed by the nearby University of Washington. The Arboretum was designed by the Olmstead Brothers of Massachussets, whose father, landscape architect Frederick Law Olmstead, laid out New York's Central Park. Tucked away in one corner of the Arboretum is the lovely Japanese Garden, tended by volunteers. It is the scene of many outdoor Japanese weddings.

(Opposite) Southeast of downtown Seattle is a beautiful forest surrounded by water. This is SEWARD PARK, a finger of land on Bailey Peninsula that juts out into Lake Washington – 277 acres used for picnicking, swimming, hiking and biking.

The campus you see below is that of LAKESIDE SCHOOL, where the well-to-do send their progeny for intellectual refinement. It is coeducational with a student population of 675 from grades five through twelve. Located in north Seattle, edging the city limits at 145th street, Lakeside has a computer center, dining hall, gymnasium, field house, and a performing arts center, and the Middle School and Upper School have libraries totalling 30,000 books. Its relatively small campus accommodates four athletic fields. Its illustrious graduates are too many to list here, except to say that Craig McCaw and three of his brothers, all Lakeside grads, went on to found McCaw Cellular Communications, a nationwide power in the industry. A 1971 graduate was Paul Allen, co-founder of Microsoft and owner of the Portland Trailblazers basketball team. Allen's good friend and Lakeside's most famous grad, is thirtysomething Bill Gates, the other founder of Microsoft who still runs the software colossus and is reputedly one of America's richest men.

(Opposite) Inside the city limits of Seattle are 83.2 miles of prime salt and freshwater shoreline property where people build expensive homes. Perhaps the choicest is this finger of land called WEBSTER POINT on Lake Washington. It is located just a few hundred over-water yards from the Husky football stadium. Jim Owens, a famous and winning UW coach, once built a home here. Students remarked that he would walk to work on water.

FISHERMEN'S TERMINAL: They are still a strong, tough people, these descendants of early Northwest immigrants from Scandinavia, Greece and other European countries. Here at Fishermen's Terminal, a public facility owned by the Port of Seattle, more than 700 vessels settle in for rest and rehabilitation. They include tiny trawlers, gillnetters, seiners, longliners, crabbers and huge trawlers. They are the North Pacific fleet, which supplies more than 50 percent of fish taken by American fishermen. They harvest no fewer than 24 kinds of fish, including the lordly salmon — sockeye, chum, Coho and Chinook. This fleet ranges from the California coast, northward into the Gulf of Alaska and the Bering Sea. Dangerous, hard work, to be sure. The death rate for U.S. fishermen is seven times the national average for all workers.

But an old fisherman's credo says it best: "The worst day of fishing is still better than the best day in an office."

In the foreground, lower right, is one of the few railroad roundhouses to be found anywhere.

(Opposite) THE CHITTENDEN LOCKS. Very few in Seattle call these busy locks, joining Puget sound with Lake Union and Lake Washington, by their right name. In Seattle, they are the "government locks" or the "Ballard Locks," after the community in which they raise and lower boats. Almost nobody refers to them as the "Hiram Chittenden Locks." This is sad. Hiram Chittenden was a remarkable man, a brigadier general, West Point graduate assigned to the Army Corps of Engineers. The locks, which opened in 1916, equalized the levels of Puget Sound, Lake Union and Lake Washington.

All that greenery, all that virtue, all that intellectual firepower. Here among the trees is the one-time FOREST RIDGE CONVENT, a Seattle landmark since 1907. Literally thousands of Catholic girls were given a strict, quality education here until 1964. Then it was sold to the Seattle Hebrew Academy, which amounts to a sort of ecumenical full circle. It is still a Seattle landmark at the north end of Capitol Hill.

(Opposite) Markedly the most prestigious (and most beautiful) of all Seattle golf courses, public and private, is the SEATTLE GOLF CLUB, established in 1900. The number of playing members, 805, is carefully controlled to avoid overcrowding. The course, with its aged trees and immaculate fairways, is 6,527 yards in length. The Seattle Golf Club adjoins The Highlands, a forested enclave populated by the city's very well to do. Its clubhouse, in the far left corner, is an active and prized social center. About 25 per cent of Highlands residents are active members.

THE HIGHLANDS lies just within the northern city limits of Seattle. The adjoining Seattle Golf Club is no longer part of The Highlands Corporation, but the founding of the region's most beautiful course, in 1908, led to the development that now numbers more than 95 estates in a 360-acre wooded compound that requires nothing less than one acre per mansion. The late William Allen who, as president of Boeing, launched the jet age in commercial air travel, once lived here. "Don't come in here to live," Allen advised an associate, "unless you can afford to hire gardeners to do your work for you."

"Privacy! privacy!" — the credo of Seattle's rich, especially the Highlands. One can drive over its miles of narrow roads and ancient bridges and never see a house. Trees, shrubbery and world-class rhododendrons are everywhere. As one female resident explained, "I always take off my swimsuit in my pool. Why not? I'm protected by three fences." There are guards and gates and private police. One Highlands home burned to the ground because the firemen got lost trying to find a road to the blaze.

The Highlands, while a private sort of national park, is only one of Seattle's several enclaves for the rich or merely well-to-do. "In Seattle," a UW sociologist once said, "there are so many beautiful areas of the city that it's a little difficult to flaunt your wealth." As one privacy-prone Highlands matron sniffed, "Fools and their money are soon invited everywhere."

Located at the north end of Lake Washington, KENMORE AIR HARBOR is a rest and rehabilitation center for 120 Seattle-based seaplanes. It is the largest seaplane base in the United States, excepting possibly for Alaska. Kenmore's aircraft parts department does more than $1 million in annual sales. Its flight school trains more than 250 pilots per year. Most of these planes are owned by Seattle's comfortably well off, who fly to Canada for fishing vacations. Kenmore's own fleet of 20 seaplanes fly into the San Juans, Canadian fishing lakes and dozens of water destinations. Its business clientele includes state agencies, the Applied Physics Laboratory and the Department of Defense. Kenmore was founded in 1946.

DISCOVERY PARK, once a military establishment (Fort Lawton), is located adjacent to the upper middle class Magnolia Bluff residential area. Seattle city fathers deeded the Discovery Park area to the U.S. military in 1896. The military used it sparingly (except for World War II) and jealously until 1972, when the area was deeded back to the city. The rather attractive white, circular buildings you see here have nothing to do with high tech or art. It is a sewage treatment plant on what is called West Point.

(*Opposite*) INGLEWOOD, a hilly, private and somewhat difficult course, is located near the northern tip of Lake Washington. In the background is Kenmore Air Harbor, the largest haven for the city's many sea-planes.

What was once a Catholic seminary is now ST. EDWARD STATE PARK, located on the Northeast shore of Lake Washington. Some 316 acres of church property were deeded to the State of Washington. In addition to public access and recreation, St. Edward State Park is now a full-use facility with playing fields, a daycare center and a drug and alcohol treatment center.

(Opposite) This string of ancient and spavined boats at the mouth of the SNOHOMISH RIVER form a breakwater for logs being towed to Everett sawmills. This practice of using old boats as a breakwater began at the turn of the century. About 30 years ago, someone discovered that one of these discards was the Equator, a yacht used by Robert Louis Stevenson during his Polynesia years. The Equator was towed away with high hopes of historical restoration, but nobody came up with the money. The Equator is now sheltered in a waterfront shed, while the other hulks continue to do their humble duty.

Frontiersman Andrew Jackson, our seventh president, would probably emit howls of profane outrage at the thought of having anything so effete as a golf course named after him. But this is JACKSON PARK MUNICIPAL GOLF COURSE, named after Andy, near the city's northern limits. Since its opening in 1930, it has become one of the most heavily played courses on the West Coast. Above is a 1939 view of Jackson Park.

The city of EVERETT, with a population of 57,000, is a 30-minute drive north of Seattle. Most of its workforce is employed at the huge, nearby Boeing factory at Paine Field. The city is flanked by mountains and, in this photograph, you see majestic Mt. Baker in the background. Everett's 2,000-slip marina makes it the second largest marina on the West Coast, surpassed only by Marina Del Rey in California.

A high-level NASA photo gives some idea of the size of Boeing's huge plant near Everett. The runway that launches giant Boeing 747s and somewhat smaller passenger jets on their maiden flights can be plainly seen from this elevation.

BOEING PLANT. Take off your hats, you devotees of foreign trade balance – in this picture you are looking at the No. 1 exporter in the U.S. at Paine Field, just north of Seattle. Perhaps just as important, you are viewing the world's largest building by volume – 472 million cubic feet of space. (See the Guinness Book of World Records.) Out of these giant doors roll billions of dollars worth of Boeing planes – the giant 747, the 767 and soon the 777. The building covers 282 acres, and the workers get around on company bicycles or electric go-carts. A typical 747 is assembled from 1,500 suppliers from 29 countries and 49 states. The place is alive with foreign airline representatives awaiting delivery. When told that the distance from one end of the building to the other was 492 meters (538 yards), a Chinese official beamed and said, "Yes, it is a very long Par 5."

This shot takes a bird's eye look at the TULALIP CASINO, a prosperous operation, controlled by the Tulalip Tribal Council. One of approximately 160 tribal gambling ventures in America, it is the second such casino in Washington State – the first being the Lummi Casino near Bellingham. Four more are in the planning stage. Trained by Las Vegas professionals, the tribal members make up about about two-thirds of the casino's 150 dealers. The Tulalip Casino draws 500-600 gamblers during the week, with 1,000 or more coming to gamble on weekends. In addition to getting a remarkable number of tribal members off welfare, the Tulalip Casino, just off I-5 near Marysville, about 30 miles north of Seattle, has helped build a dental clinic, and the tribe expects to build a new community center for tribal elders.

CEDARCREST, a municipal golf course in Marysville, is a short, easy to play (no sand traps, but small greens) layout – distinguished by one thing. This lovely course was the growing-up backyard of Ann Quast (now Sander), one of America's greatest woman amateur golf players. Ann began her career at Cedarcrest, which her parents owned, as a 3 1/2-year-old toddler. She grew up to win the Women's Amateur Championship in 1958, 1961 and 1963. She played on the U.S. Curtis Cup team in 1958, 1960, 1962, 1968, 1974, 1984 and 1990. She played two years (1966 and 1968) on the Women's World Cup Team and was Women's Western Amateur Champion in 1956 and 1961. Ann and her husband, Steve, lived outside London for a while. She journeyed back to England in 1980 and won the Ladies' British Amateur Open title.

Each spring 60 miles north of Seattle comes a burst of color in the fertile SKAGIT VALLEY that others have likened to "an explosion in a paint factory." This is the Skagit Valley Tulip Festival. There is more than tulips – iris and daffodils, and literally thousands of people. The event, complete with busses, traffic jams, state police and volunteers, probably outdraws any single sports event held in Seattle's Kingdome. Display gardens and greenhouses burst with color. The attendant Chamber of Commerce hi-jinks also features the Great Skagit Duck Run in which 7,000 to 10,000 rubber ducks are turned loose by their owners (they cost $5 apiece) and take off down the river.

(Opposite) Although much of its workforce is employed by Boeing, EVERETT still does much business in lumber. These logs, sheltered by a breakwater near Everett's waterfront, will be towed by tugs to nearby sawmills. Weyerhaueser's first large mill was built in Everett.

THE WHIDBEY ISLAND NAVAL AIR STATION, located at the north end of the island, is the home of all Navy electronic tactical jamming aircraft. It is a training center for the A-6 "Intruder" attack bomber squadrons. Search and Rescue aids civil authorities for operations in the Pacific Northwest. Many of Whidbey's personnel served in the Desert Storm gulf war, and in the background you will see the painted message near the runway: "Welcome Home."

(Opposite) Just north of Seattle is the longest island (60 miles) in the contiguous U.S. WHIDBEY ISLAND is a mix of forested hills, farmland, rocky beaches and a rich history of Salish Indians, English explorers and traders. It is the only island in Puget Sound accessible by car (over the Deception Pass bridge visible in the lower center of the photograph). This bucolic island also hosts the Whidbey Island Naval Air Station – home of the Navy's electronic warfare flying squadrons.

ROCHE HARBOR on San Juan Island is one of the Northwest's most popular summer vacation resorts. Its harbor shelters thousands of boaters each year and the resort has its own private air strip for fly-in visitors from the Puget Sound region. Canadians and Americans gather here during the first week of July to honor their country's friendship – on Dominion Day, July 1, and on our own July 4.

(Opposite) San Juan Island is a favorite boat-gathering spot for Canadian and American pleasure boaters. FRIDAY HARBOR'S waterfront moorages accommodate some 20,000 boats annually. The town of Friday Harbor has a U.S. Customs station for people arriving by boat and plane from Canada, many from Victoria, only a short distance away. The late great author, Ernest K. Gann, wrote several of his novels and flying adventure books at his ranch near Friday Harbor.

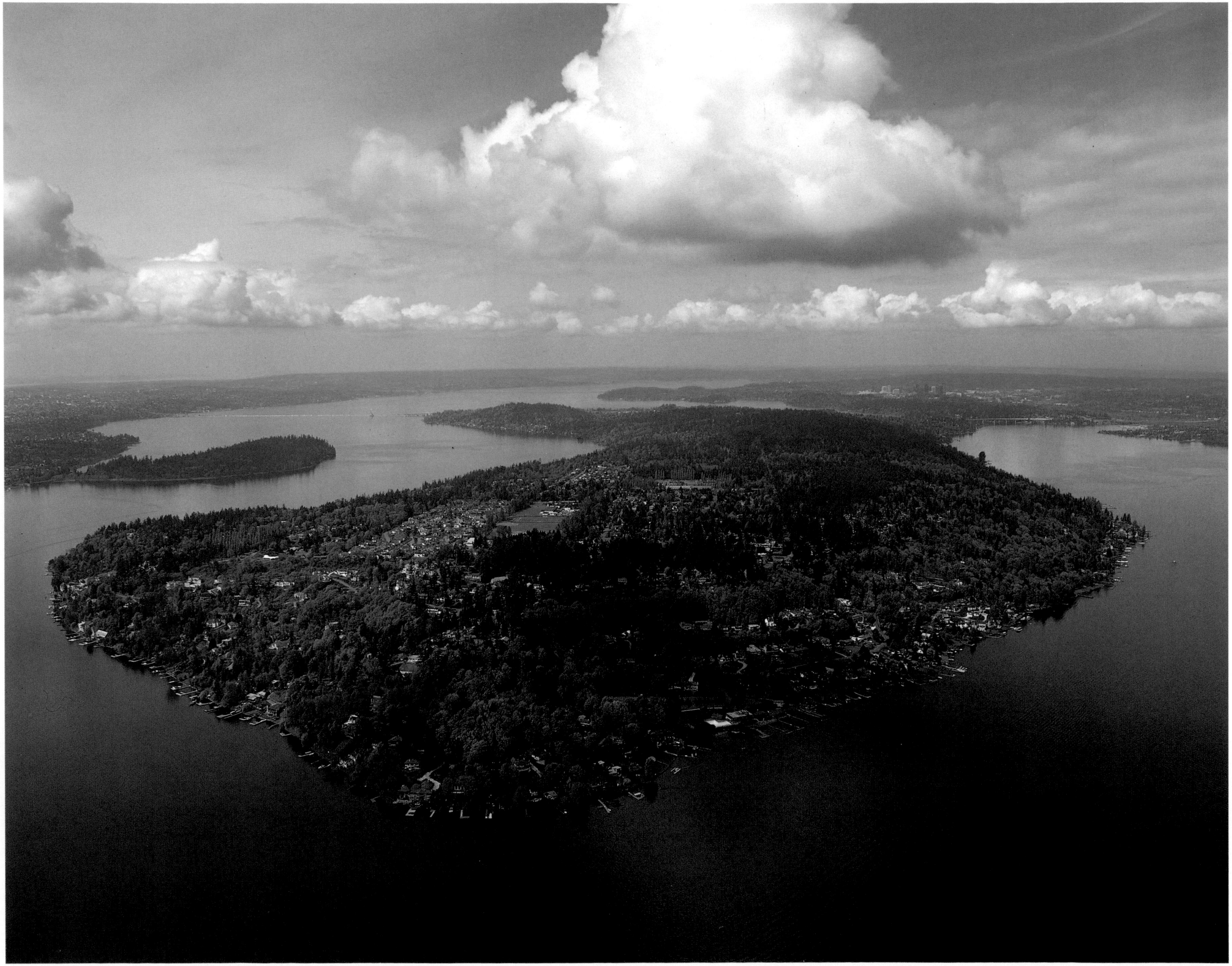

With convenient access via bridges to the commercial centers of Seattle and the Eastside, MERCER ISLAND in Lake Washington is a serene enclave for the wealthy — known principally to non-islanders for the excellence of its high school basketball teams and the loftiness of its real estate prices. The latter are especially dear on the south end of the 5,000-acre island, where residents are farthest from Interstate 90's traffic noise and nearest to treasured views of Mt. Rainier. Typically Seattle, part of the floating bridge to Mercer Island sank during a 1991 storm. The new parallel floating bridge manages to handle heavy traffic, but rumor had it that during its building, contingency plans were laid that, should a section break away, planes from McChord Air Force Base would sink the runaway section with bombs. Islanders have been denied this spectacle, so far. Mercer Island is an incorporated city, yet Seattleites think of it as a city within their city.

There is nothing soft about MICROSOFT'S dominance of the computer software industry. Microsoft grosses more than $3.2 billion in yearly sales. This is the Microsoft "campus" in Redmond, east of Seattle. It is composed of 30 buildings on 212 acres, totaling 1.6 million square feet of office space. Because it is Microsoft and owner Bill Gates wants it that way, the 30 buildings are "networked" by 7,000 miles of cable. In the 30 buildings is an on-campus population of 5,345.

(Opposite) Once remote farmland, then a vacation area, then a waterfront retreat for the wealthy, BELLEVUE has grown into the state's fourth largest city with a skyline that can be seen from Seattle across the lake.

OVERLAKE GOLF & COUNTRY CLUB can be reached easily from Seattle via the Evergreen Point floating bridge. But it's an Eastside pride, located in Medina. The club opened in 1927 and many Seattle hackers rode the ferry from Leschi to get there. Sunk by the Great Depression, Overlake became a horse breeding and Hereford cattle farm; Overlake was re-acquired and rebuilt and opened again in 1953. With 400 golfing members, paying some $80,000 to join, Overlake sits on valuable land in pristine prosperity. The exclusive community of Hunt's Point juts into Lake Washington at the right. Above is a 1932 photograph of the same area.

The statue between sunshine and shadow in ISSAQUAH, a small town east of Seattle, is that of a man named Vladimir Ilyich Ulynov. You might know him better as Nicolai Lenin. Lew Carpenter, a resident of Issaquah with a puckish sense of humor and a little money, bought the statue of Lenin when he found it in a storage yard of a foundry in Slovakia. At a cost of some $40,000 he had the 16-foot high, seven-ton bronze likeness shipped to Issaquah. Lenin looks noble and fierce, but he's just an artifact in Carpenter's back yard.

(Opposite) More than 100 feet up, higher than Niagara, SNOQUALMIE FALLS spills its namesake river down toward the Snoqualmie Valley, a short drive east of Seattle. The Falls, a landscaped park and picnic facility, is also the home of the upscale Salish Lodge. The Cascade range's twin peaks is in the background.

RADAR LAKE. You would not think, would you, that Puget Sound, which gets water from all directions, would need any man-made lakes. But there are reportedly some 20 private lakes (some of them just glorified irrigation ponds) devoted mostly to water skiing. This is Radar Lake, east of Seattle, which was not named after some sterling pioneer. It is owned by the Radar Electric Co. No public water skiing.

(Opposite) SEATTLE AND ELLIOT BAY at twilight, as seen from east of Lake Washington, the the sun peeking through the dark, often black, rain-bearing clouds. Painters and photographers alike are enraptured by the city's grays and greens, its raw beauty never diminished by modern marinas and bustling docks.

Here at the southwest corner of Boeing Field is the MUSEUM OF FLIGHT with its Great Gallery where more than 40 full-sized aircraft are on display, more than 20 of them suspended from the roof. Behind the Great Gallery is the historic "Red Barn" where William E. Boeing built his seaplane, the "B & W," Boeing's first airplane, on Lake Union. Boeing Field was the site of Seattle's first powered airplane flight in 1910. A flying replica of the B & W is among the museum's attractions, which also include a working replica of the wind tunnel used by the Wright Brothers. On the tarmac to the right of the museum is America's first jet bomber, the B-47. The museum, founded in 1983, contains a full-sized theater for lectures and a collection of aviation documents and is a mecca for aviators from around the world.

(Opposite) Towering in the distance beyond Runway 31 right at BOEING FIELD is Mt. Rainier in its full majesty. All Northwest pilots know that by taking off and climbing on the runway heading, 130-degrees, they would eventually fly directly over the summit of Rainier.

As you can see from the 1933 photo, BOEING FIELD was home to old Army Air Corps biplanes. A modern view of Boeing, now virtually an urban airport, shows it as a testing site for Boeing jets being delivered to most of the world's airlines. The old Army Air Corps tie-down space is now taken up by hangars; Boeing Field is home to hundreds of modern aircraft, from corporate jets to small single-engine planes.

BOEING CAMOUFLAGE. Seattle and the Northwest were afraid of Japanese bombers during World War II. Barrage balloons covered Bremerton, and Boeing went to great pains to camouflage its B-17 and B-29 manufacturing plants. Note the small village on the left (opposite). It is all fake, a "neighborhood" constructed atop an airplane plant. Here is how the camouflaged area looks today.

BOEING-RENTON. The city of Renton, at the south tip of Lake Washington, is home to a Boeing manufacturing site. It was on this runway, opposite page, that the great Dash-80, America's first commercial jet, took off for its initial test flight in 1955. The Dash-80 had more than 1,000 clones — the celebrated Boeing 707, which not only shrank the planet but helped make Seattle famous as a sophisticated metropolis in the U.S.'s far Northwest corner. Standing next to the original Dash-80, now owned by the Smithsonian Institution, is famed test pilot A.M. "Tex" Johnston, who took the great plane on its maiden flight. It was Johnston who slow-rolled the plane before a hugh crowd on Lake Washington in 1955, thus putting Boeing's and Seattle's signatures on the age of jet travel.

JEFFERSON PARK GOLF CLUB. There are 10 private and 48 public golf courses in King, Pierce and Snohomish Counties — and this is Jefferson (named after the famous Tom) the oldest public course in Seattle. It sits high atop Beacon Hill with a sweeping view of the City. Jefferson, which opened in 1915, was designed by the famed Olmsted brothers of Boston who had such a big effect on Seattle's topography, including the beautiful Lake Washington Boulevard.

(Opposite) This curious golf course, near KENT, a town south of Seattle, is surrounded by the Green River. The river is probably close to blockage from lost golf balls.

With permission for his helicopter to hover over the runway, Bob Cameron was able to shoot this splendid landing of a C-141B Starlifter, a military transport plane based at McCHORD AIR FORCE BASE near Tacoma. In addition to the famed C-141B Starlifters, McChord recently became home to the Air Combat Command's 354th Fighter Squadron — composed of 24 A-10 Thunderbolt II aircraft, with more than 500 Air Force members.

(Opposite) Like everything else in our procreative age, now-crowded facilities were once considered "too far away" by commerce fans. So it was with SEATTLE-TACOMA INTERNATIONAL AIRPORT, 13 miles from the city's downtown. Says one Seattle Port official, "What we have is a very short turnaround time between seaport and airport. It is the quickest of all West Coast ports." Sea-Tac, as the natives call it, is well-designed and remarkably efficient. It handles more than 15 million passengers and about 300,000 metric tons of air cargo each year. Sea-Tac services 38 airlines, including 13 international passenger and 13 all-cargo carriers. And once again, as local patriots never tire of telling you: Sea-Tac is equidistant between Tokyo and London with about nine hours flying time to each city. And the Seattle harbor makes it a world leader in the movement of sea-air cargo.

(Opposite) The immensity of the WEYERHAEUSER timber empire (run from its headquarters pictured here) can scarcely be grasped by any single imagination. The offices below, on I-5 outside Tacoma, are open and accessible (no private offices) and the company employs 39,000 people in the U.S. and Canada. Weyerhaeuser was 57th on the Fortune 500 list for 1992, based on 1991 sales of $8.7 billion. Its forest products come from Washington, Oregon, North Carolina, Mississippi/Alabama, Oklahoma/Arkansas and Georgia. It manufactures almost anything having to do with wood from 13 locations in America. Its principal business is the growing and harvesting of trees. The company likes to say that 98 per cent of all Weyerhaeuser lands are always growing trees. In addition to its U.S. private timberland (5.7 million acres) the company has long-term licensing rights in Canada on nearly 16.5 million acres. Anyone who has ever used a toothpick probably owes something to Weyerhaeuser.

This mostly wood geodetic design is the colorful TACOMA DOME, opened in 1983 and now averaging 325 "event days" a year. Much smaller in capacity than Seattle's Kingdome, the Tacoma structure concentrates on ice hockey, high school sports, wrestling, thrill sports and boxing. Tacomans like to point out that "our dome is much prettier than Seattle's," a somewhat irrelevant but happy fact. In the far distance steam rises from a waterfront pulp mill.

THEA FOSS WATERWAY fronts Tacoma's downtown waterfront. In the background is the Tacoma Dome. The waterway was named after Thea, a heroic, strong-willed lady who built Foss Tug and Barge into one of the nation's largest such firms; she started with a rowboat. Thea Foss was the model for "Tugboat Annie," a 1933 film starring Marie Dressler and Wallace Beery. A remake of "Annie" came out in 1940, starring Marjorie Rambeau as Tugboat Annie. Two prominent supporting actors in this film were Ronald Reagan and Jane Wyman.

(Opposite) Nestled between Interstate-5 and the east shore of American Lake is the oldest golf club west of the Mississippi. According to the Official Golf Guide 1899, published by J.M. Thornburn & Co., New York, the TACOMA COUNTRY & GOLF CLUB opened in 1894. The course was the inspiration of transplanted Scotsmen, employed by the Balfour Guthrie Co. Today it's a beautiful course of championship caliber, but back then this new game mystified Tacoma's residents. The Scots sent away to their homeland and imported 30 golf sets, handmade by Forgan, the famous club maker. The Port of Tacoma customs agent, baffled by these ancient Scottish instruments, finally admitted the clubs to Tacoma and listed them as "farm tools."

TACOMA'S UNION STATION, now an historical landmark, was built in 1911 and was jointly owned by Union Pacific, Great Northern and Northern Pacific. The city of Tacoma acquired the abandoned station for $1 in 1984. It is now refurbished and open to the public; adjoining it is a new annex, now a U.S. District Courthouse.

STADIUM HIGH. What looks like a French hotel, even a French castle, is not anything like a hotel, but it started out that way. Back in 1890 Tacoma Land Co. and Northern Pacific Railroad began building what they hoped would be the world's or at least Tacoma's, most spectacular hostelry, called Tourist Hotel. The economic panic of 1893 halted construction and the building sat vacant for five years. Then, with a stroke of genius, the city acquired the building and turned it into a high school in 1903. It is called Stadium High because it fronts on a stadium that sets in a ravine once called "old woman's gulch." The stadium has hosted hundreds of football games and survived such natural disasters as earthquakes and the oratory of evangelist Billy Sunday, William Jennings Bryan and Warren G. Harding, among others. Downtown Tacoma can be seen in the background.

Puget Sound has dozens, perhaps hundreds of picturesque bays, inlets, harbors, islands and semi-islands. Here is a semi-island, known as MAURY ISLAND, with Quartermaster Harbor and Vashon Island on the left. Maury, although given the status of an island, is actually joined to much larger Vashon Island by a narrow sandspit and a black-topped road. Maury is one mile wide and five miles long.

(Opposite) Yet another Northwest learning instdition is located on expensive waterfront property. This one includes some 902 men in its all-male student body, with a service staff of 500. The residents number among them some of America's most skilled artisans in the fields of fraud and thuggery. What looks like a college campus, or a high tech plant, is the McNEIL ISLAND PENITENTIARY, some 4,400 acres in all. It has a long history dating back to 1870 when it became a territorial jail and admitted its first federal prisoner in 1875, a man convicted of selling liquor to Native Americans. McNeil Island was formally dedicated as a federal penitentiary in 1907. By 1981, it was leased by the State of Washington and in 1983, ownership of the island was transferred to the state. Its modern enrollment never seems to decline.

(Opposite) SOUTH SEATTLE COMMUNITY COLLEGE, on an 82-acre hilltop in Southwest Seattle, overlooks Elliott Bay. It is one of 32 community and technical colleges in Washington State. This one was opened in 1970 and now has a student body of 6,800, 35 per cent of which are minority and foreign-born, representing nearly 100 different cultures.

ALKI POINT, part of West Seattle, was where the first settlers in this region landed. They beheld a centuries-old forest of giant trees so tall they "swept the stars." Logging felled nearly all the giants. But Ferdinand Schmitz, a banker and realtor, and his wife, Emma, recognized the forest heritage of Puget Sound would one day be lost. So they deeded a wooded ravine to the city in 1909 "for the purpose of preserving forever a reminder of the magnificent cathedral of forest" that so awed the first settlers. This ravine is known as Schmitz Park and can be seen at center right.

THE BREMERTON NAVAL SHIPYARD, a 45-minute ferry ride from downtown Seattle, is a favored storage and repair station for the U.S. Navy. The 1934 photo is matched with today's facility. The modern clutter includes several nuclear submarines being decommissioned, along with stored carriers and destroyers. Among the Bremerton Navy Yard's distinguished guests are the carrier USS Nimitz and the battleship USS Missouri which, in 1945, made considerable history in Tokyo Bay.

Bob Cameron's aerial photo of the BANGOR
NUCLEAR SUBMARINE BASE on Hood Canal, a few
miles north of Bremerton, caused no uproar among
security-conscious Navy personnel. Much of what goes
on here, above and below the water, is top secret. Yet
Puget Sounders are quite laid back by the deadly presence
of Bangor. Pleasure boaters know the rules well — if a
submarine is sighted, boats must keep 1,000 yards'
distance.

(Opposite) EAGLE HARBOR. The town of Winslow, the entry to Bainbridge Island, is yet another of Seattle's many bedroom communities. Indeed, much of Bainbridge Island itself, 12 miles long, four miles wide, is a Seattle commuting destination. Washington State ferries carry more than 23 million passengers a year. The busiest route is Seattle to Winslow, 22 trips daily, a crossing of Elliott Bay and Puget Sound that takes 35 minutes. The ferries enter Eagle Harbor, a famed recreational boating area, one of the most diverse (and polluted) harbors in the area.

AGATE PASS BRIDGE, completed in 1950, frees Bainbridge Island from total dependence on ferries by connecting the island with the Kitsap Peninsula, west of Puget Sound. The Agate Pass waterway has a swift current and narrow waist, only 300 yards wide. Few agates are to be found here. The passage was named after a man name Agate (Alfred T.), an artist with an 1841 surveying expedition. The clearing on the right is Memorial Cemetery where Chief Seattle is buried.

This white sand beach on the north end of VASHON ISLAND gives the sweep and flavor of Seattle. In the distance is a large freighter entering Elliott Bay, the Seattle skyline beyond. Vashon Island, both a vacation retreat and homes for the city's ferry commuters, is where the well-known K-2 skis are manufactured.

(Opposite) Perhaps the most scenic of all Puget Sound boat refuges is GIG HARBOR, just outside Tacoma, where the per capita pleasure boat ownership is incredibly high. Gig Harbor itself, with a population of only 2,500, is alive with tourist-pulling shops, restaurants and galleries.

With a population of 17,000, PORT ANGELES is the largest city on the Olympic Peninsula. It is a busy harbor, protected by Ediz Hook, visited by lumber and fishing boats. Port Angeles, easily reached by ferry from Victoria, B.C., is where huge ships stop and are boarded by special Puget Sound pilots who guide their charges through the complex waters of Puget Sound to Seattle, Tacoma and Everett.

This otherwise unremarkable town on the Olympic Peninsula is famous only for having less rainfall than its nearby neighbors. The town is SEQUIM (pronounced "skwimm") which lies under the so-called "blue hole" of incoming rain clouds off the Pacific. It gets only half of Seattle's 34 annual inches of rain. It is a favorite Northwest retirement community.

(Opposite) Tourism accounts for most of PORT TOWNSEND's prosperity. This small town on the north-east corner of the Olympic Peninsula was once (in the late 1800s) a bustling commercial seaport. Its wealthy townsmen built many fine, historic mansions, many of them now bed-and-breakfast retreats. Port Townsend, which has more Victorian-style buildings to be found anywhere north of San Francisco, thrives on boutiques, antiques, galleries and scenery.

The coastline of the UPPER OLYMPIC PENINSULA fronts on the Strait of Juan de Fuca. Below is a community breakwater with sections of the sunken Hood Canal floating bridge standing by to be used for more breakwaters. In the distance is a great cloud bank off the most westerly part of the United States. Also shown is a picturesque volcanic outcropping, common to that rugged coastline.

(Opposite) TATOOSH ISLAND. There it is, friends and neighbors – the most northwestern part of the contiguous United States. Contiguous means not counting Hawaii and Alaska. Tatoosh Island stands alone, a lonely outpost, battered by waves from the not-so-pacific North Pacific ocean, home to a lighthouse that warns ships headed toward Puget Sound to stay well out into the Strait of Juan de Fuca. It is the final outpost for a visit to Seattle and the Northwest. Everything west of here is ocean and Japan.

The somehow soft, yet wild, northern beginning of the rugged range of Olympic Mountains. Viewed at dusk, much of this range is part of OLYMPIC NATIONAL PARK — some 908,720 acres of America's "last wilderness."

(Opposite) A twilight view of famous LAKE CRESCENT in the Olympic National Park, west of Puget Sound and Seattle. Crescent is a freshwater lake, some 600 feet deep and 8½ miles long. The lake is the stuff of Indian legends and home to the famous Beardslee trout, a subspecies of sizeable fighting qualities.

SEATTLE'S CENTRAL WATERFRONT was once a solid, hard-working place of cargo ships and longshoremen. But with containerized cargo, the "working" waterfront moved south to Harbor Island. Today the old waterfront is a series of restaurants, tour boats, gizmo galleries and tourist-pleasing souvenir shops; it is one of Seattle's favorite leisure attractions, as hordes of natives and tourists walk along its once-tough precincts. This scene is part of Seattle's "Maritime Week," held each May. Also part of the festivities are the tugboat races shown on the opposite page and the next three pages.

These are the great PERCHERONS OF PUGET SOUND, powerful boats that push, pull and tow the huge freighters entering Seattle waters. They range in horsepower from 1,000 to 4,300 and from 80 to 120 feet in length. Annually, some 42 tugboats in three classes of boats — small, harbor class and unlimited mastodons — compete in a series of three 1.8-mile races along Seattle's waterfront during Maritime Week in May.

Tugboating is a way of life on Puget Sound and good crews are valued. The old-time movies about "Tugboat Annie" with Marie Dressler and Wallace Beery were shot in ELLIOTT BAY, and indeed, the Harbor class winner receives the Tugboat Annie Trophy. These black aquatic draft horses are a common sight in Seattle, festooned with obsolete automobile tires for use as bumpers.

Ferry passengers use a transportation system on PUGET SOUND that is more than 100 years old. It is the largest ferry system in the United States. Washington's water-borne commuter fleet carries more than 23 million passengers a year and makes more than 400 trips a day. The ferries annually carry more than nine million vehicles of all kinds — cars, trailers, recreational vehicles and giant over-the-road trucks. Thousands of residents in outlying communities (Bremerton, Bainbridge Island, Vashon Island, Whidbey Island) are true working commuters, much like the people who ride New York subways. Yet 60 percent of passengers each year, tourists and locals, ride the ferries for pleasure. The ferries happen to be Seattle's leading tourist attraction.

Today's great ferries are the progeny of what was called a "mosquito fleet" that plied Puget Sound during the 19th Century. These steam-driven craft were big, little, haphazard and brutally competitive in the early years of the 1900s; these hundreds of private enterprise craft got their nickname when a local newspaper writer said in describing the city's harbor: "At five o'clock in Seattle, the little commuter steamers scurry off to their destinations like a swarm of mosquitoes."

Today's modern jumbos and "super class" ferries carry 160 to 200 vehicles and 2,000 to 2,500 passengers. By local custom many ferries are christened with Indian names — Hiyu (meaning "plenty"), Kalama ("pretty maiden"), Klahowya ("greetings"), Quinault ("river with a lake in the middle"), Tyee ("Chief"), Walla Walla (tribe of eastern Washington), and Sealth (Indian spelling of "Seattle").

Shown here are two ferries on Puget Sound with the 76-story Columbia Seafirst Center looming in the foreground.

Ferries, a tug pulling a raft of logs and sailboats mingle freely on PUGET SOUND, where pleasure craft and workboats have long accommodated one another.

These shots were taken not from an airplane, a helicopter or a lunar orbiting station. It was taken by Bob Cameron, an 82-year-old marvel with a camera, who climbed all the way up to the peak of the 250-foot high KINGDOME roof to photograph this SEATTLE MARINERS baseball game with his wide angle lens. On the next page, also from high inside the Kingdome, he captured this action shot of the NFL SEATTLE SEAHAWKS getting ready to play the San Francisco 49ers. The Seahawks won, 30-0, a result that sent hometowners into paroxysms of joy.

Seattle takes its football seriously — some say too seriously. These views of the 70,000-seat UNIVERSITY OF WASHINGTON STADIUM were taken shortly after the Pac-10 champion Huskies were penalized for recruiting violations. Thousands come to Husky games by private and chartered boats. TV networks covet its panoramic setting, with Lake Washington to the east. The older view is of a game in the 1920s, when the stadium's capacity was 30,000.

Because of frequent blizzards on Mt. Rainier, skiers have moved to nearby CRYSTAL MOUNTAIN, shown here with Rainier in the background. Crystal is the best of the Cascade ski resorts.

(Opposite) There is a special Seattle affection for the "DUWAMISH" and the "CHIEF SEATTLE," and with good reason. These are the fireboats that protect most, if not all of Seattle's waterfront — and they will not be forgotten, even when no fires burn. On special occasions the "Big D," or the Duwamish, and her sister combat veteran, Chief Seattle, go out into Elliott Bay and spray tons of water in the air. The scene is spectacular.

This is a typical, smashing view of Seattle in summer — the hydroplane race course on LAKE WASHINGTON with Elliot Bay and the Olympic Mountains in the distance. Even the city's giant orange cranes, the Kingdome and the downtown skybusters are included in this remarkable, panoramic shot from a helicopter. Thousands of boat-owners pay moorage fees to ring the race course and many of them party all night before the Sunday races.

(Opposite) HYDRO RACES. The so-called "thunderboats," or unlimited hydroplanes, annually shoot up "rooster-tails" as they race around an oval course on Lake Washington. Some 200,000 or more people, ashore or on pleasure boats, view the exciting spectacle of roaring hydros reaching speeds close to 200 miles per hour. It is all part of Seattle's summer Seafair celebration.

A NASA photo from space of MT. RAINIER dramatically portrays the mass of the mountain and its giant glaciers. More than 35 square miles of ice, including 26 officially named glaciers and numerous icefields, cover Rainier's upper slopes and summit dome. Six major glaciers flow down directly from the crater rim to well below timberline. The mountain is so massive it creates its own weather. Though Rainier seems placid, it is, in fact, an active volcano, and massive mudslides can result from interior heating, an event that takes place every generation or so.

(Opposite) Like a great Northwest icon, mighty MT. RAINIER, 14,411 feet high, can be seen for hundreds of miles. It has an almost religious majesty for the region. Rainier has claimed the lives of dozens of climbers, yet people come from all over the world to scale its summit. It was at Rainier's Paradise Inn that Otto Lang, the great Austrian instructor, established America's first ski school using the Hannes Schneider technique. Mere children have climbed it; the oldest climber was 81. Several veteran climbers, including Lou and Jim Whittaker, have gone on to climb Mt. Everest and K-2. Hundreds have climbed Rainier, but as Lou Whittaker says, "The mountain itself tells you when to stay away." A fair number of men and women (nobody knows how many, or will reveal their identity) have climbed Rainier, then made love at the summit. They are unofficial members of what is called the "Rim Club."

A big festive Seattle celebration, aptly called BUMBERSHOOT, is held every Labor Day weekend. The festival at Seattle Center features the visual and literary arts, along with music, dance and theater. Some 200,000 attend each year. It's a long way, as generations span, from Seattle's hob-nailed-boots beginning.

(Opposite) Visitors say to Seattle natives, "But you talk as if you OWN the mountain!" And so they do. MT. RAINIER is omnipresent on all clear days and its elegant, towering image is part of the entire Northwest scene.

147

The beginning of Seattle's boating season is highlighted by the OPENING DAY PARADE from Portage Bay, through the Montlake Cut, and on into Lake Washington by hundreds of pleasure boats. Most spend the night before as a bobbing flotilla of cocktail and beer parties.

The opening of the boating season always occurs on the first Saturday of May and has been a Seattle tradition and the city's most colorful display of nautical enthusiasm for 73 years. But it sometimes rains on our best parade, as it did here in 1993. Yet the shivering thousands never lose heart, and thousands more line the shore of the cut, past the ceremonially raised Montlake Bridge, to cheer on dozens of racing crews, including Washington's own, both men and women, and crews from as far away as Boston and Germany. Opening Day Parade boats include everything from multi-million dollar yachts to kayaks. Seattle enjoys water and wetness.

The view (opposite) looks east toward Lake Washington. The views to the right look west from the lake and south from the lake toward downtown.

One of the Northwest's corniest jokes is, "We've grown too big for our bridges," another way of saying we have trouble with them. The first to go was "Galloping Gertie," the first Tacoma Narrows span that was twisted into falling wreckage during a high wind in 1940. Another big wind collapsed and sank the Hood Canal Floating Bridge in 1979. And in 1978, a ship going up the west waterway of the Duwamish River past Harbor Island crashed into the West Seattle drawbridge, which stuck up in the air, a helpless immovable wreckage (as shown here). People in nearby West Seattle were more or less cut off from the city until alternate routes could be arranged. Today, as shown opposite, the new WEST SEATTLE BRIDGE soars far above the waterway. Finally, in 1990, another storm sank the I-90 Bridge, now handsomely restored.

Footnotes: When the Tacoma Narrows Bridge went down, it was discovered that the insurance agent pocketed the premiums and never notified his company. He went to prison for this deliberate oversight. And the skipper in the West Seattle Bridge disaster was 82-year old Rolf Nessen, who mysteriously disappeared somewhat later. Capt. Nessen's problem, it was found, was not navigational but marital. His wife was convicted of his murder.

WEST SEATTLE BRIDGE

While the original I-90 BRIDGE was being rebuilt to lie alongside the new span, a storm in the winter of 1990 filled some of the pontoons upon which the bridge floated with water, causing part of the bridge to sink and other parts to break away. This view shows what remained. Opposite is a 1993 view showing the new bridge on the right and the rebuilt original bridge, both needed to accommodate the ever increasing traffic between Seattle and the burgeoning Eastside of Lake Washington. At bottom is Mercer Island, which I-90 crosses, leading oldtimers to call the span the Mercer Island Bridge.

I-90 FLOATING BRIDGE

A roaring February windstorm in 1979 sank more than half the HOOD CANAL BRIDGE, a span connecting Kitsap Peninsula with the Olympic Peninsula to the west. What remained of the bridge is shown opposite. The late Sen. Warren Magnuson of Washington, then a Senate power, obtained funds to rebuild the bridge. Magnuson's Senate colleagues eventually took to kidding him about the Northwest's frequent need to rebuild sunken and broken bridges. "You people," one said, "seem to have a lot of trouble with your bridges out there." The rebuilt span is especially busy in summer, when visitors flock to the glorious Olympic Peninsula's mountains, wild beaches, old-growth forests and rain forest.

HOOD CANAL FLOATING BRIDGE

"Galloping Gertie," the original TACOMA NARROWS BRIDGE, came to her inglorious end in 1948 – a twisted wreckage that whirled in a high wind and then collapsed into Puget Sound. This photo is probably the most prized action picture in Northwest archives. Since Northwesterners don't give up when it comes to spanning their waters, a new bridge over this part of southern Puget Sound replaced Gertie and, as shown opposite, has proved more durable.

TACOMA NARROWS BRIDGE *(Galloping Gertie)*

Here are more scenes of Seattle lit up at Christmas. Note the boats festooned with holiday lights. This is part of an annual waterborne Christmas parade.

(Opposite) In addition to miles of water, Seattle is a city of inexpensive and plentiful electricity. The whole town seems to light up in winter nights. One of its more festive sights is the SPACE NEEDLE, decorated with lights during the Christmas holidays.

A final, grand view of Seattle at twilight, overlooking MAGNOLIA BLUFF and Elliot Bay Marina. Dark rain clouds make their way from the west, casting their shadows on Puget Sound.